THE BEAUTY OF A DISCIPLINED LIFE

THE
Beauty
OF A
DISCIPLINED LIFE

REBECCA GATES

ChariotVICTOR
PUBLISHING
A DIVISION OF COOK COMMUNICATIONS

Victor Books is an imprint of ChariotVictor Publishing,
a division of Cook Communications, Colorado Springs, Colorado 80918
Cook Communications, Paris, Ontario
Kingsway Communications, Eastbourne, England

12   13   14   15   16   17   18   19   20   Printing/Year   97   96

Scripture verses quoted are taken from the *Holy Bible, New International Version*
(NIV), © 1973, 1978, 1984, International Bible Society. Used by permission of
Zondervan Bible Publishers; and *The Amplified Bible* (AMP), © 1965, by Zondervan
Publishing House; and from J.B. Phillips: *The New Testament in Modern English*, Re-
vised Edition (PH), © J.B. Phillips, 1958, 1960, 1972, permission of Macmillan
Publishing Co. and Collins Publishers.

Recommended Dewey Decimal Classification: 223.7
Suggested Subject Heading: BIBLE, O.T.—PROVERBS

Library of Congress Catalog Card Number: 86-63101
ISBN: 0-89693-248-6

CONTENTS

This study guide on the Book of Proverbs is designed for use as both a personal resource and as the basis for group study. If you are using this book for personal study only, then the information which follows should get you started on your way to effective personal Bible study. If, on the other hand, you are planning to use this as the basis for group study, you will want to refer to the Leader's Guide at the end of this book where specific suggestions for using this study in a group setting can be found.

Each study in this guide is divided into three parts—Personal Journey, Wisdom's Path, and Daily Pilgrimage. In the Personal Journey section you will find a series of questions designed to help you examine a discipline found in the Book of Proverbs. Always take time to read the Bible passage through, thoughtfully. Pray for wisdom and the Holy Spirit's guidance as you answer the questions. The goal of each study is to see what the Bible has to say, so you won't need any commentaries or expert resources. You may choose to spend one *day*, or one *week*, on each study depending on how much time you can devote to the discipline of Bible study. More important than how much time you spend studying Scripture at one given time is how consistent you are in your study practice. Is it a *daily* discipline for you?

After completing the Personal Journey section, take time to read Wisdom's Path. This part of the lesson will amplify the basic themes of the discipline you are studying so that you will see how God's truth can be applied to your daily walk with Jesus Christ.

The Daily Pilgrimage feature of this series of studies is designed to help you keep a daily journal throughout the study. Take time to record your personal reactions to the Scriptures suggested for your day-to-day consideration. Read, meditate, pray, record. Let God speak to you and let Him know what you are hearing Him say as you make it a practice of writing down your thoughts.

May you cultivate that basic ingredient for successful living—self-discipline—as you make your way through *The Beauty of a Disciplined Life*.

CHAPTER ONE

THE DISCIPLINE OF

❧ PERSONAL JOURNEY ❧

Read Proverbs 1–4.

1. The first four chapters of Proverbs focus on the importance of acquiring wisdom. It is interesting to note the many facets of wisdom that are unveiled in these four chapters. Like a beautiful diamond with many points, wisdom is multifaceted. As you read, jot down a list of all the words that appear to be parallel or synonymous with the word *wisdom*. Try to find as many as 15 parallel words and/or phrases. Seen together, these words and phrases give us a more complete picture of the meaning of wisdom.

2. What actions listed in Proverbs 2:1-4 lead us to the fear of the Lord and the knowledge of God?

3. The person who finds wisdom is described in Proverbs 2:7-8. What are some of the words used to identify such a person?

4. Wisdom is described as being more profitable than silver, yielding better returns than gold, being more precious than rubies, and

more exciting than hidden treasure. Its benefits are listed throughout Proverbs 3. Search out the value of wisdom from the following Scripture references. Then express in your own words the main idea of each verse.

Proverbs 3:2

Proverbs 3:4

Proverbs 3:6

Proverbs 3:8

Proverbs 3:10

Proverbs 3:23

Proverbs 3:24

Proverbs 3:26

5. Wisdom not only promises valuable benefits; it also helps us avoid pain caused by foolish actions. What are some of the pains that a woman could avoid by acquiring wisdom? Refer to specific examples found in Proverbs 1–4.

6. Read Psalm 119:97-112. What actions did the psalmist take to attain understanding or wisdom?

7. Self-discipline is a voluntary action that one takes to secure a benefit and/or to avoid pain. What act of self-discipline does Psalm 119:97-104 suggest to you?

8. To whom must our search for wisdom lead? Study 1 Corinthians 1:20-24 and Colossians 2:2-3 before answering this question.

9. Reread all or parts of Proverbs 1–4, substituting the name of Christ for "wisdom" and its parallel forms. What insights did this exercise give you? Write down some of the most exciting things you learned and be sure to share these new insights with others.

10. The Word of God is a storehouse of wisdom on a variety of subjects. Quickly read through each of the following Scripture passages and summarize in one or two words the topic each passage addresses.

   Matthew 6:19-21

   Romans 13:1-7

   Ephesians 5:22-28

   1 Thessalonians 4:13-17

11. In what specific area of your life do you need wisdom right now? What steps (voluntary actions) will you take to acquire wisdom for this situation?

❧ WISDOM'S PATH ❧

What are your feelings after studying Proverbs 1–4? Are you invigorated and eager? Do you feel challenged? Perhaps you feel a bit overwhelmed? Women's lives have become increasingly complex and fragmented by hectic schedules, financial burdens, marital stress, and relational problems. The resulting lack of self-esteem and numerous fears and anxieties drive women either to high levels of stress, exhaustion, and depression or to a determination to seek wisdom from God.

Your participation in this study is an indication of your desire to seek wisdom from God. There are three important things to remember about the process and discipline of acquiring God's wisdom.

It is a lifelong process. For many years I was impatient to achieve spiritual maturity. I thought of wisdom as a destination at which I ought to arrive. I became frustrated because I seemed to make so little progress toward my destination. I wanted so much to "grow up" and get on with living a mature, Christian life.

Recently, I was able to spend several days with my godly, 87-year-old grandmother. Through the time I spent talking with her, I came to realize that my maturation process will continue until the day I die. In her increasingly fewer lucid moments, my grandmother expressed her desire to have God's wisdom in facing the remaining days of her life. And all this time, I thought she had already "arrived"!

I sensed in a new way how much I need to seek God's wisdom every day of my life. Every new set of circumstances, every new stage of life will require that I be involved in the lifelong discipline of seeking God's wisdom.

It is a painful process. Perhaps you have heard the phrase, "no pain— no gain." These words aptly describe the process of acquiring wisdom. Hebrews 12:11 says, "No discipline seems pleasant at the time, but painful. Later on, however, it produces a harvest of righteousness and peace for those who have been trained by it."

Be wary of those who would state or imply that a Christian can expect a pain-free life. The discipline required in your search for God's wisdom will always involve some pain. The pain, however, produces a harvest of righteousness and peace.

It is a necessary process. In spite of the pain and the time involved, the acquisition of wisdom is essential to each of our lives. As you have seen in your personal study, Proverbs discusses the issue as a choice between life and death. We must be convinced that both the benefits of finding wisdom and the consequences of rejecting it, surpass by far the momentary pain of the process of acquiring wisdom.

Wisdom has always been a highly desirable quality. The quest for wisdom was the basis for the first temptation and eventual fall of mankind. The serpent presented the fruit of the tree as the pathway to wisdom. However, there was no wisdom in the serpent's advice because eating the fruit was a direct contradiction of God's instructions.

Today there exists an abundance of counterfeit wisdom. Television, books, and magazines offer advice to millions who seek counsel for living in this complicated age. In order to weed our way through all of the counterfeit wisdom in our society, we must know the characteristics of God's wisdom. James 3:17 lists the characteristics of God's wisdom.

It is pure. We can be sure that any counsel or advice that violates God's standards for moral purity is not wisdom from God. To follow such a path is to court disaster. But beyond just moral purity, God's wisdom promotes purity of heart and motive. Any thought or action that contradicts God's holiness should be weeded out of our lives.

It is peace-loving. Those who are wise will seek to preserve peace where it exists and restore peace where it no longer exists. The wise woman will endeavor to create an atmosphere of calmness and serenity in her home. Through organization and decor she and her family can develop an environment that is conducive to peace. Through her joyful and calm spirit she can bring God's peace to everyone around her.

Most of us can find opportunities to preserve and restore peace in our neighborhoods. We can demonstrate our commitment to peace by refusing to listen to or pass along gossip, helping to clear up misunderstandings, and performing simple acts of kindness.

It is considerate. Heavenly wisdom is not rude. It is considerate of the other person's time and feelings. It does not persist in self-promoting conversation, but provides a listening ear. It is not consistently late, for it recognizes that other person's time is valuable. It pays as much attention to the feelings of a child as to the feelings of a person of worldly rank or importance.

It is submissive. The submissive aspect of wisdom is clearly described in the *Amplified Bible's* Version of James 3:17, "[It is willing to] yield to reason." God's wisdom will enable us to yield to reasonable requests from others. It also gives us the incentive to live under the lordship of Jesus Christ.

> I appeal to you therefore, brethren, and beg of you in view of [all] the mercies of God, to make a decisive dedication of your bodies—presenting all your members and faculties—as a living sacrifice, holy (devoted, consecrated) and well pleasing to God, which is your reasonable (rational, intelligent) service and spiritual worship" (Romans 12:1, AMP).

It is full of mercy and good fruit. Acting in accordance with God's wisdom means to readily extend forgiveness to all who offend us. Such action frees us from the bonds of bitterness. It also helps us understand and receive God's unconditional acceptance of us. Heavenly wisdom goes a step beyond forgiveness though, by including the offer of goodness to others. Generosity and cheerfulness will be typical of the actions of a wise woman.

It is impartial and sincere. Impartiality is an important quality in parenting, in work situations, and in church life. In addition to this, wisdom is sincere. A wise person need not hide any part of his or her person from another. There is nothing to hide in a sincere person.

What are your circumstances today? Are you perplexed and bewildered by problems of enormous significance? Are you facing the "dailies" of life that cause you to search for resources to cope? God's wisdom is available for the asking.

> If any of you lacks wisdom, he should ask God, who gives generously to all without finding fault, and it will be given to him (James 1:5).

> Wisdom is supreme; therefore get wisdom. Though it cost all you have, get understanding. Esteem her, and she will exalt you; embrace her, and she will honor you. She will set a garland of grace on your head and present you with a crown of splendor (Prov. 4:7-9).

❦ DAILY PILGRIMAGE ❦

SUNDAY: Psalm 111:10

God says

I respond

MONDAY: Proverbs 2:6

God says

I respond

TUESDAY: Daniel 12:3

God says

I respond

WEDNESDAY: Romans 11:33

God says

I respond

THURSDAY: Ephesians 1:17

God says

I respond

FRIDAY: Colossians 2:3

God says

I respond

SATURDAY: James 1:5

God says

I respond

THE DISCIPLINE OF

CHAPTER TWO

Marital Faithfulness

🐚 PERSONAL JOURNEY 🐚

Read Proverbs 5; 6:20-35; and 7.

1. Proverbs 5:1-6 contrasts two approaches to the marriage relationship. Verses 1 and 2 illustrate a wise approach to marriage. Verses 3-6 illustrate a foolish approach. Using the following questions compare the wise approach to the marriage relationship with the foolish approach.

How do the lips of the two persons described in these verses compare? (Compare v. 2b to v. 3.) What command is given to the son in verse 1? How does this command contrast with the description of the adulteress in verse 6? What will be the result of our obedience to the command in verse 1? (v. 2) What happens to the person who follows the example of the adulteress? (vv. 4-5)

2. Extramarital affairs are often portrayed in an idealized, romantic light. This is only a disguise. Read each set of verses below. Indicate the disguise and the reality of an illicit affair as it is portrayed in each verse.

DISGUISE	REALITY
Proverbs 5:3	Proverbs 5:4
Proverbs 6:25	Proverbs 6:26
Proverbs 7:21	Proverbs 7:22-23

3. Throughout Proverbs we are reminded of the result or the end of certain actions and attitudes. Look up the following references and summarize the situation or behavior and the outcome or end discussed in each. Note whether the end is positive or negative.

REFERENCE	SITUATION	THE "END" (+ or -)
Proverbs 14:12-13		
Proverbs 19:20		
Proverbs 20:21		
Proverbs 23:17-18		
Proverbs 24:14		
Proverbs 24:19-20		

4. Proverbs 7:6-23 is a dramatic example of what can happen if we don't stay clear of trouble. In what ways does the young man in the passage go against the instruction given in Proverbs 5:7-8?

   What are the results of the young man's encounter with temptation? (vv. 22-23)

5. In what kinds of situations might you be tempted to sin sexually?

What are some practical actions you can take to overcome or avoid these temptations?

6. The delights of sex in marriage are referred to in Proverbs 5:15-20. There is joy, blessing, and benefit in the healthy marriage relationship. List some of the blessings you have experienced in your marriage relationship.

7. Faithfulness should not be limited to the sexual aspect of marriage. Unfaithfulness in any area of marriage violates the principle of oneness demonstrated by Christ's love for His Church (Eph. 5:24-32).

   Read Song of Songs 8:6-7 and compare it with 1 Corinthians 13:4-8. Then write out some practical ways you can improve the quality of your marriage.

8. What do you choose to do in the coming week to demonstrate your desire to contribute to marital faithfulness?

❧ WISDOM'S PATH ❧

The subject of marital faithfulness is extremely relevant to our lives today. Social and cultural change, as well as the sexual revolution, have had devastating effects on marriages. Divorce and marital infidelity have increased at an alarming rate. Magazines, television, and movies unashamedly champion lifestyles that violate God's principle of marital faithfulness. Because Christians' marriages are not exempt from these pressures, Proverbs' emphasis on developing discipline in the area of marital faithfulness is pertinent to us. The message of Proverbs 5 can be summarized with three headings: the disguise of infidelity, the distresses of infidelity, and the delights of fidelity.

The disguise of infidelity. You uncovered this disguise in your personal study. J. Allen Peterson has called it *The Myth of Greener Grass* in his book on the subject. Why do so many people fall prey to the myth? It appears from Proverbs 5 that infidelity begins with simple temptations. Through our eyes and ears enter the stimuli that overwhelm good judgment and plant the seeds of infidelity.

Part of the charm of an illicit affair lies in the apparent mystery, excitement, and rapture that cast a romantic aura over otherwise good judgment. Remember that the aura is very different from the reality. Let the reality serve as a deterrent to unwise action and as an encouragement to pursue godly behavior.

Once we are aware of the subtle temptations of infidelity, we must exercise the discipline necessary to avoid entrapment. This discipline may mean restricting your television viewing, canceling magazine subscriptions, or spending less time listening to certain kinds of music. Be aware of the messages you are listening to, and avoid anything that might be subtly urging you toward infidelity.

On the positive side, you might want to increase the amount of time you spend in God's Word. Determine to read uplifting books. Listen to music that lifts up God and expresses the praise of your heart to Him.

The distresses of infidelity. If the gross reality of adultery was not enough to deter a person, the specific distresses that are found in Proverbs 5 should be further persuasion. The early stages of an affair often hide problems that underlie infidelity. The harsh reality of the internal guilt and the tangled web that ensnares the participants is often hidden by candlelight, roses, and romance. However pain and despair are inevitable results of immoral behavior.

Interestingly, much of the advice regarding marital faithfulness in Proverbs is directed to men. The woman in these verses is portrayed as the aggressor. Stop and consider this observation for a moment. The woman is described as having a smooth tongue, lips, and speech; a seductive appearance; and a wandering spirit. These descriptions suggest areas in which we, as women, need to exercise discipline. The conscientious Christian woman should evaluate her behavior in light of these descriptions. We should not be naive about the "vibes" we may be giving off through our words, appearances, clothing, and lifestyles.

In considering the distresses associated with infidelity, remember that all infidelity is not outward. Jesus reminded his followers that to sexually desire a person other than your marriage partner is to commit adultery in the heart (Matt. 5:28). The seeds of temptation that often lead to unfaithfulness are sown in the mind and imagination. We need to discipline our thoughts and guard our minds from impurity. As 2 Corinthians 10:5 says, "We take captive every thought to make it obedient to Christ." If this is an area in which you need help, commit some of the verses from the *Daily Pilgrimage* to memory.

The delights of fidelity. Proverbs 5 is not all gloom and doom. Verses 15-20 contain language that has been described as imaginative and erotic. This language illustrates that the sexual experience is in its very essence pleasurable. However, outside of the Song of Songs such language is rare. Scripture, more often, seems to stress the complementary aspect of marriage, emphasizing both the necessity of procreation and the need to protect the sanctity of sex.

There is joy, blessing, and benefit in the healthy marriage relationship. To ignore the sexual delight in marriage is to misunderstand God's intent and to force human passion to seek other outlets. Clear instruction about the sexual aspect of marriage can be found in 1 Corinthians 7:2-5. Three points are clearly seen in these verses. First, both partners in marriage have definite and equally important sexual needs that should be met in marriage. It is important that you understand the needs of your partner. Do you know what they are? Are you able to discuss them? Have you identified your own sexual needs? Have you communicated them to your husband? Communication is an important part of a healthy sex life. *Marriage Encounter* provided my husband and me with a tool to improve our communication skills. There are other resources available. Be the one to take the first step to improve communication in your marriage. You won't regret it!

A second truth from 1 Corinthians 7 is that it is the responsibility of the wife to meet her husband's needs. Fatigue is a common complaint of women today. However, fatigue should not keep us from the responsibility and delight of meeting the sexual needs of our husbands. Be creative in overcoming fatigue (or any other barrier). Exercise discipline in getting the proper amount of sleep and exercise that you need to maintain an attractive and healthy body. This will contribute greatly to the enthusiasm level you have for this exciting activity.

The third truth is that a healthy Christian life and a satisfying sexual relationship in marriage go together. Lack of satisfaction sexually makes a person vulnerable to temptation. Also, a Christian woman who meets the needs of her unsaved husband may help guide him to personal faith in Christ through her behavior (1 Peter 3:1).

Although our focus has been the sexual aspect of marriage, faithfulness is a necessity in other aspects of marriage as well. Demonstrate your commitment to your spouse in good times and bad, sickness and health, poverty and wealth. Keep your conversation about your spouse loyal and positive. By words and actions evidence the love that you felt certain of on the day you said, "I do!"

🐛 *DAILY PILGRIMAGE* 🐛

SUNDAY: Genesis 2:24

   God says

   I respond

MONDAY: 1 Corinthians 7:5

   God says

   I respond

TUESDAY: Ephesians 5:3

   God says

   I respond

WEDNESDAY: Ephesians 5:21-22

    God says

    I respond

THURSDAY: Ephesians 5:33

    God says

    I respond

FRIDAY: Titus 2:4

    God says

    I respond

SATURDAY: Song of Songs 8:10

    God says

    I respond

CHAPTER THREE

THE DISCIPLINE OF

PERSONAL JOURNEY

Read Proverbs 6:1-19; 31:10-31.

1. Proverbs 6:1-5 describes a person who has assumed the responsibility of another person's debt. Solomon advises people to get out of such situations quickly. What actions does Solomon urge for a person in this situation?

How do the two metaphors in verse 5 help emphasize the danger of procrastination?

2. In the second example (Prov. 6:6-11), Solomon uses the ant to illustrate the principle of wisely investing one's energy. In what ways does the ant demonstrate the three following aspects of disciplining one's energy? (Prov. 6:6-8)

Set priorities (knowing *what* to do).

Learn time management (determining *when* to do things).

Be a self-starter (taking responsibility for your own actions).

3. In Proverbs 6:9-11, what does the sluggard do while the ant works?

What will be the result of the sluggard's laziness?

4. Proverbs 6:16-19 illustrates seven attributes of someone who has not learned to direct his energies. Since these are described as things that God hates, we can be sure that the opposite attributes of these seven would be good ways to direct our energies. Make a list of the seven bad attributes and then beside each attribute list its opposite.

(1)

(2)

(3)

(4)

(5)

(6)

(7)

5. The virtuous woman of Proverbs 31:10-31 is the perfect example of a disciplined person. Character is the basis of her actions (v. 10), and the basis of her character is the "fear of the Lord" (v. 30).

   Read Proverbs 31:10-31 and make a list of the action words (verbs) that describe the woman. Then, beside each action word (verb) write the corresponding object (i.e. selects—wool and flax).

6. Read through Proverbs 31:10-31 again, this time looking for the kinds of activities or roles which the woman of Proverbs 31 assumed.

Make a list of those roles/activities in the left-hand column below. Then beside each of this woman's roles, jot down one corresponding role/activity of your own.

Her Roles/Activities	My Roles/Activities
Example: v. 20—cared for the poor	*food-pantry volunteer*

7. Read Proverbs 24:30-34. Write down the words or phrases used to describe the sluggards vineyard.

8. Read the following verses and summarize what each one has to say about disciplining our use of time and energy.

Galatians 4:18

Philippians 3:13-14

1 Thessalonians 4:11-12

Hebrews 12:1

❧ WISDOM'S PATH ❧

The sixth chapter of Proverbs has quite a bit of advice regarding the discipline of energy. One dictionary defines energy as "vigor or power in action; the capacity for action or accomplishment." The practice of disciplining one's energy keeps a person youthful in spirit, sound in body, and productive of mind.

Women who have not learned to discipline their energies usually behave in one of two ways. The first is the woman who can't seem to get going. Her capacity for action and accomplishment is seemingly non-existent or at least very low. Rest assured, there is hope for the woman with a low energy level. She can learn to discipline her energy to accomplish more.

The opposite extreme is the perpetual-motion type of person. This person says, "It seems like I go, go, go, but I don't get anywhere!" Haste *does* make waste. Confusion surrounds this type of person. There is hope for her too. This person can learn to discipline and focus her energy more efficiently and effectively.

The low-energy person. How closely I identify with this problem! By nature I am lazy and undisciplined. My experience in dealing with this problem has taught me a valuable lesson: Energy produces energy! Since I have learned that, I understand why my energy level either spirals downward or soars upward from one day to the next. The less I do, the less I feel like doing. The more I do, the more I feel like doing. Think about this for a minute:

> *You don't do what you do because you feel like you do;*
> *You feel like you do because you do what you do.*

(You might need to read it out loud to really understand it.)

Of course, consistently low energy levels can also be caused by physical problems. Often though, the problem is more closely related to laziness and/or procrastination. As I write these very words my latest confrontation with procrastination is only three hours behind me. Rising early this morning, I determined to begin writing this chapter—after I had my cup of coffee. However, thumbing through a decorating magazine while I sipped my coffee, I was reminded of the half-bath I was eager to redecorate. I walked into the bathroom and put a fingernail under the wallpaper at a seam. Sure enough! The wallpaper could be easily removed. I proceeded to strip the paper from the walls. This precipitated a minor cleaning job requiring broom and dust pan. By the time I was finished with that task, my husband and son had returned from their early morning golf outing and the day was in full swing. Finally, I almost literally picked myself up by the back of the neck and placed myself at the desk. Through an act of my will and by God's grace I determined to complete what I needed to do.

Obviously this was not the first time I have had to deal with procrastination and I strongly suspect it will not be the last. I believe that growth is a journey, not a destination. For this journey I have discovered five steps that help me get around the roadblocks of procrastination and laziness.

First, confess procrastination and laziness as sin. Remember James 4:17, "Anyone, then, who knows the good he ought to do and doesn't do it, sins."

Second, establish priorities and manage your time. That is the lesson we can learn from the ant (Prov. 6:6-8). Invest significant amounts of time only in activities that are high priorities in your life.

Third, learn to focus on the task to be done. This requires self-discipline. Put on blinders to the distractions around you. Forget the past. Don't worry about the future. Focus on what needs to be done.

Fourth, do the job regardless of how you feel. Don't worry if you don't feel enthusiastic about a task you need to complete.

Fifth, limit sleep and television watching. Avoid using these activities as escapes from doing a job.

The perpetual-motion person. In trying to compensate for my habit of procrastination, I have occasionally gone to the other extreme. A perpetual-motion person is typified by:

> *Activity without accomplishment;*
> *Frenzy without fulfillment;*
> *Dizziness without direction;*
> *"Go" without goal.*

Remember that balance is the goal of the disciplined life. These suggestions might prove helpful to a person struggling to control and focus her energies.

☐ Plan for and observe a daily quiet time. Begin by setting aside a short period of time (5 minutes) that you can be alone each day. Choose a time and place that will minimize your chances of being interrupted or distracted. Spend the first few moments in silence, letting your mind and body unwind. Then, talk to God about the upcoming day.

☐ Establish priorities and learn time management. Write down the things you know you have to get done. Number them in their order of importance. Then, complete one task at a time, beginning with the most important.

☐ Make a habit of finishing what you start.

☐ Review your activities at the end of each day. Did you successfully follow your "game plan"? Or did you make some mistakes along the way? What changes do you need to make to avoid repeating the same mistakes day after day?

A lifestyle of balanced energies. The most exciting insight I have gained from the woman of Proverbs 31 did not come from reading a book about her. Rather, I gained the most exciting insight from a Bible study similar to the one in the *Personal Journey* section of this lesson. First, I underlined all the action words (verbs) in Proverbs 31:10-31. This woman was definitely not lazy! She didn't procrastinate either. Next, I underlined all the direct objects in the passage twice. For example: She *considers* a *field* (v. 16). The direct objects demonstrate the purpose and direction in her activities. Finally, I drew circles around the descriptive words (adjectives and adverbs). Words such as strong, eager, and profitable are used to describe the quality of her life and efforts.

Every time I read over these verses, I notice something new about this model woman. I am challenged to control my schedule so that I take time to know God and to walk in His wisdom. I see the need to budget my energy so that I not only spend enough time on myself and my personal needs, but I also have time and energy to invest in the lives of people around me. I get enthused about broadening my interests and increasing my expertise in certain areas. I am convicted about the need for focus and planning. By God's grace, I want to be like the woman of Proverbs 31.

Now is the time to move closer to the balance God is showing you. Discipline your energies to accomplish the purpose God has for you. Don't settle for less than the best. Determine to focus your time and energy to complete each task and move closer to your goals.

🦋 DAILY PILGRIMAGE 🦋

SUNDAY: Proverbs 12:24-27

God says

I respond

MONDAY: Proverbs 13:4

God says

I respond

TUESDAY: Proverbs 14:23

God says

I respond

WEDNESDAY: Proverbs 18:5

    God says

    I respond

THURSDAY: Proverbs 21:5

    God says

    I respond

FRIDAY: Proverbs 24:30-34

    God says

    I respond

SATURDAY: Proverbs 15:19

    God says

    I respond

THE DISCIPLINE OF

Quietness

🐚 *PERSONAL JOURNEY* 🐚

Read Proverbs 8, 9, and 10.

1. Listening is certainly an important skill to learn. Children who know how to listen perform better in school. Adults who know how to listen have better relationships and are generally more likely to succeed. How much more important it is to learn to listen to God.

   Read Proverbs 8 and make a list of the verses that contain a plea to listen (hear or hearken in the *King James Version*).

2. What benefits does Proverbs 8 suggest will be gained by those who listen?

3. What are some things that might keep a person from listening to God?

4. What role does quietness play in listening to God?

5. One very important point is that no one can speak and listen to someone else at the same time. Read Proverbs 10 and notice the contrast between the words (or speaking habits) of the wise man and the words (or speaking habits) of the fool. Complete the following chart comparing the godly person and the foolish person:

Verse	Godly Person	Foolish Person
8		
10		
11		
13		
14		
18		
19		
20		
21		
31		
32		

6. Was Jesus a quiet person? Did He lead a quiet life? Before answering these questions, look up the following Scripture references. Then summarize what each verse has to say about Jesus' life.

Matthew 14:13

Matthew 14:23

Mark 1:35

Mark 6:31

Luke 5:16

Luke 6:12

What did you learn about Jesus that you didn't know before?

7. The following questions may give you some insight into how to incorporate the discipline of quietness into your life. Spend some time carefully thinking through each question.

What distractions consistently keep me from being quiet in God's presence?

How might I eliminate distractions?

In what area of my life am I most easily agitated?

How can I face that situation more calmly?

Do my family, friends, and acquaintances perceive me as a gentle, quiet person?

Do I need to make some changes?

❧ WISDOM'S PATH ❧

Quietness is a rare commodity in our world today. Noise pollution has become a serious problem requiring study and recommendations by environmentalists. Some cities are even proposing laws banning the playing of loud music in public places.

Close your eyes for a moment and listen. What sounds do you hear? I hear the noise of a youth group playing volleyball outside the back window. There is the steady hum of a fluorescent light punctuated frequently by the sounds of cars zooming past the front of the building. Occasionally the beep-beep of a horn interrupts the soft, persistent chirping of birds singing their evening songs. Quiet? Not here.

Quiet means to be free of noise, hushed, calm and unmoving, still, restful, soothing, characterized by tranquility, serene and peaceful. Do you know of *any* quiet place? Noise has become such an accepted feature of our everyday lives that we are usually uncomfortable when things get too quiet! I have caught myself many times getting into the car and automatically reaching for the radio. If, while speaking on the telephone, you happen to get put on hold, music is often played to keep you from being alone. We don't really know how to be quiet.

In order to learn how to be quiet, we need to do three things. We need to discover the true nature of quietness. We need to see the need for quiet. And we need to discipline ourselves to experience quiet.

Discovering the nature of quietness. It is important to know the nature of quietness. Silence has two spheres: inner and outer. It is very important that we learn to develop the inner sphere because inner quietness is the foundation of outer quietness. Yet, it is so easy to neglect the inner part of our lives because it is so intangible.

Jesus knew and demonstrated the importance of the inner sphere. He often withdrew to lonely places and prayed. Centuries ago, the desert church fathers would go into the desert for extended periods of time in order to cultivate inner peace. They knew the importance of external quietness for developing the inner world of quietness. It takes discipline however, to cultivate the silence of the soul. Gordon MacDonald in his book, *Ordering Your Private World,* likens the inner sphere to a garden. He says the garden is the place where the Spirit of God comes to share wisdom, to give affirmation or rebuke, to provide encouragement, and to give direction and guidance. To keep the garden a place of order and tranquility, MacDonald suggests four disciplines: solitude and silence, listening to God, reflection and meditation, and prayers of worship and intercession.

Apart from the cultivation of inner quietness, it is difficult to maintain order and quietness in our external lives for any length of time. We live under the "tyranny of the urgent," where the quiet promptings of the Holy Spirit are overwhelmed by our hectic lifestyles and the demands of others on our time. All too often we attempt to bring order to our worlds by trying to manipulate external activities. Unless alterations to our outer worlds are prompted by order in our inner lives, the effects will be temporary at best.

Discerning the need for quiet. One reason we need quiet is to get to know God. Psalm 46:10 directs us to "Be still, and know that I am God." Through meditation and reflection we learn to know God.

A second reason we need quiet is to learn how to live wisely. Proverbs repeatedly associates noise and much talking with foolishness. It is a sign of discipline and wisdom to control our words and order our lives.

A quiet spirit is a necessity for good interpersonal relationships. People who control their words are better listeners. They are not so apt to express anger and respond in haste in tense situations.

A final reason to cultivate inner and outer quietness is that it is consistent with righteous living. "The fruit of righteousness will be peace; the effect of righteousness will be quietness and confidence forever" (Isa. 32:17). A quiet life demonstrates to outsiders the inner peace we experience in Christ (1 Thes. 4:11-12). Also, a quiet life demonstrates the result of godly and holy living (1 Tim. 2:3). Life lived from the inside out gives support and credence to the faith we profess.

Discipline our lives for quietness. It is not enough to know why we need quiet. It is not enough to wish our lives were more orderly and quiet. We need to discipline ourselves, our time, our environments, and our lifestyles to be conducive to inner and outer tranquility.

First, decide whether or not quietness is a priority. It does not matter that someone we admire makes a priority of quietness. It does not matter that we think quietness ought to be more important to us. We must firmly establish quietness as a personal priority. Only then will we be able to put aside the secondary matters that interfere with our higher priorities. Once established as a priority, quietness becomes something for which we must plan.

Plan your schedule carefully to allow adequate time to practice this discipline. Schedule a quiet time into your daily routine. I have found that writing down my plan and placing a starting and ending time beside it, reinforces my intention to observe a quiet time. Also, it is helpful for me to have a general format to follow during my quiet times. I usually need some time to warm up and convince myself that I am serious about being quiet! Sometimes it takes several minutes to clear my mind of distractions. Then I proceed with plans to read the Word, meditate, and listen to God.

A principle I learned from Anne Ortlund's book, *Disciplines of the Beautiful Woman,* is "eliminate and concentrate." For my own quiet times, I find it helpful to choose an uncluttered place in which to be quiet. There are fewer things to distract me in an uncluttered place. In fact, eliminating clutter is a useful principle to follow in establishing a relaxing, peaceful, environment in your home. To minimize the distractions in your environment, it may be beneficial to use the same place every day for your time of solitude and silence. After several days, your surroundings will not distract you nearly as much as if you were moving from place to place.

While some people may be strong enough to shove aside distracting thoughts, I feel more comfortable writing down thoughts that need attention or future action. Sometimes these thoughts are mere distractions. Other times, the thought that seems to distract us may actually be a prompting of God's Spirit. By quickly making note of these thoughts, I am able to put them aside and deal with them after my quiet time.

All of these suggestions involve self-discipline. If solitude and silence are truly important to us, our lifestyles will be affected and changed. We will find ourselves saying no to more trivial pursuits. The pace of our lives will probably slow down. Some of the strain and stress of a hurried life will be relieved. And our ordered lives will be a confession of the beauty of the peace of God that passes human understanding.

🍂 *DAILY PILGRIMAGE* 🍂

SUNDAY: Isaiah 30:15

God says

I respond

MONDAY: Isaiah 32:17

God says

I respond

TUESDAY: Isaiah 40:31

God says

I respond

WEDNESDAY: Psalm 46:10

God says

I respond

THURSDAY: 1 Thessalonians 4:11

God says

I respond

FRIDAY: 1 Peter 3:4

God says

I respond

SATURDAY: Proverbs 9:13

God says

I respond

CHAPTER FIVE

THE DISCIPLINE OF

🐌 *PERSONAL JOURNEY* 🐌

Read Proverbs 15.

1. Throughout Proverbs there are many references to the use of the tongue. As you read through Proverbs 15 try to locate some specific instruction regarding the use of the tongue. Find all the verses that speak of the tongue or speech and record them in the appropriate places on the chart.

Verse	Positive Use of Tongue	Negative Use of Tongue

2. There is much power in the tongue. Look up and read the following Scripture references, then summarize what they have to say about the power of the tongue.

Proverbs 10:11

Proverbs 10:21

Proverbs 12:25

Proverbs 13:3

Proverbs 16:21

Proverbs 18:21

3. Look up and read the following verses. Then pick a key word or phrase that summarizes the principle taught in each verse.

Proverbs 10:21

Proverbs 12:22

Proverbs 12:25

Proverbs 15:23

Proverbs 16:24

Proverbs 25:15

4. If you had to choose one principle from the above list to work on this week, which one would it be?

5. Write down a situation where you expect to have an opportunity to use disciplined speech this week.

6. Proverbs 15:2 and 15:28 describe the speech of fools. Compare these verses with 2 Timothy 2:16 and Matthew 12:36. What do these verses teach us about undisciplined speech?

7. To what things is the tongue compared in James 3:1-9? In what way is the tongue like each of these things?

8. How is discipline of the tongue related to other areas of self-discipline? (See James 3:2.)

9. According to James 3:8, no one can tame the tongue. This is a sobering thought! What are we to do about controlling our speech? Read James 4:7-10. Make a list of the direct commands given in this passage (i.e., each phrase that begins with an imperative verb).

🐚 *WISDOM'S PATH* 🐚

She slipped a tiny piece of paper into my hand. I unfolded it and read the words printed in her seven-year-old style. "Mom, I'm sorry I bother you." Tears washed my eyes as I remembered my harsh words when she interrupted my work earlier in the day.

What a difference a word can make! What power there is in the tongue! "I said it without even thinking!" is a common expression. Unfortunately, it is often true. There seems to be a direct route between the heart and the tongue. Once spoken, words cannot be taken back. A whole forest can be set on fire by one little spark. In the same way, a marriage can be destroyed, a relationship with a child can be damaged, a church can be killed, or a reputation can be ruined by a thoughtless word. How then, can we begin to discipline our tongues or speech to be constructive forces instead of deadly weapons?

Keep in mind the holiness of God. Isaiah 6:1-8 describes the calling of Isaiah to be a prophet. Isaiah had a vision of God in His holiness, high and exalted in His temple. Isaiah's immediate response was, "Woe to me! I am ruined! For I am a man of unclean lips, and I live among a people of unclean lips." One of the angelic beings worshiping God removed a burning coal from the altar and touched Isaiah's lips with it. "See, this has touched your lips; your guilt is taken away and your sin atoned for," said the seraph.

To keep our speech clean and edifying, we need to keep before us a vision of God. The people we rub shoulders with, the television programs we see, the words we read, even in newspapers, can crowd out our remembrance of God's holiness. If you are consistently around filthy talk and blasphemous language, it is hard not to pick up the habit except by concentrating on the holiness of God.

Keep in mind the instruction of the Word of God. "My tongue was meant to praise Him" is a line from a children's song sung consistently around our house. Hebrews 13:15 instructs us, "Through Jesus, therefore, let us continually offer to God a sacrifice of praise—the fruit of lips that confess His name." As we learn to offer God continual praise, we will have less time and desire to use our tongues in any other way.

Keep in mind the judgment of God. We are so accustomed to instant rewards that the reality of God's judgment is often dimmed. Nonetheless, Jesus said, "But I tell you that men will have to give account on the day of judgment for every careless word they have spoken. For by your words you will be acquitted, and by your words you will be condemned" (Matt. 12:36-37).

It is *God's* part to *cleanse* us from all unrighteousness (1 John 1:9). It is *our* part to *keep* ourselves from unrighteousness. As that applies to the tongue, it means we are to restrain it. Consider these verses:

> *He who guards his mouth and his tongue keeps himself from calamity* (Prov. 21:23).

> *If anyone considers himself religious and yet does not keep a tight rein on his tongue, he deceives himself and his religion is worthless* (James 1:26).

> *For, whoever would love life and see good days must keep his tongue from evil and his lips from deceitful speech* (1 Peter 3:10).

Restraining the tongue requires strong self-discipline. In fact, it may take more self-discipline than most of us can imagine. James said that a person who has learned to control his tongue at all times is perfect and will be able to keep every other part of his body in check (James 3:2).

The statement in James 3:8, "no man can tame the tongue" could leave us feeling discouraged. However, it was meant to lead us back to the source of wisdom—God Himself. Jesus promised, "You will receive power when the Holy Spirit comes on you" (Acts 1:8). When the Spirit came at Pentecost, the first physical sign of His arrival was His control of the disciples' tongues. Peter who had earlier denied Christ, stood before a massive crowd and delivered a powerful sermon. The Holy Spirit used Peter's tongue to add 3,000 people to the church in one day! By giving our bodies to God as an act of worship (Romans 12:1), we can be assured that the Holy Spirit will be with us and will help us discipline our speech.

Remember: the tongue can build people up; the tongue can speak words that are perfect for the occasion; the tongue can cheer people; and the tongue can bring blessings to families, churches, neighborhoods, and the world.

❧ DAILY PILGRIMAGE ❧

SUNDAY: Matthew 12:36-37

    God says

    I respond

MONDAY: 1 Thessalonians 5:18

    God says

    I respond

TUESDAY: Matthew 15:11

    God says

    I respond

WEDNESDAY: Ephesians 4:29

God says

I respond

THURSDAY: Proverbs 31:26

God says

I respond

FRIDAY: Philippians 2:14-15

God says

I respond

SATURDAY: 1 Peter 3:15

God says

I respond

CHAPTER SIX

THE DISCIPLINE OF

Humility

✎ *PERSONAL JOURNEY* ✎

Read Proverbs 15:25—16:20.

1. Lack of self-esteem is a serious problem among women. Much has been written and said about self-esteem. However, the safest and wisest place to learn about self-esteem is from the Word of God. Read the following verses and answer this question, " What are the results of true humility?"

   Proverbs 3:34

   Proverbs 11:2

   Proverbs 15:33

   Proverbs 22:4

2. Look up and read the following Scripture references. Then summarize in a word or two what each verse teaches about the results of pride.

   Proverbs 11:2

   Proverbs 13:10

   Proverbs 15:23

Proverbs 16:5

Proverbs 16:18

Proverbs 29:23

3. The best example of true humility comes from the life of Jesus. Read Philippians 2:5-11 and make a list of the words or phrases that describe specific attitudes and/or actions of Jesus.

4. Jesus demonstrated selflessness by taking the form (nature) of man. How does this action differ from the common misconception of humility? (belittling one's self or one's abilities)

5. The "therefore" that begins Philippians 2:9 indicates a direct cause and effect relationship. What did God do as a result of Christ's willingness to humble Himself?

Compare this with Proverbs 15:33b.

6. Isaiah 14:13-15 describes the antithesis of Christ's humility. In the person Isaiah describes, we see the inborn characteristics of every

man and woman. How does this proud person demonstrate self-centeredness?

7. Self-absorption is a preoccupation with either one's perceived superiority or one's perceived flaws. What is the preoccupation of the person in the Isaiah passage?

8. What personal desire controls and motivates the speaker of the words in Isaiah 14:13-15?

9. It sometimes appears that a selfish person loves himself too much. Actually he does not love himself enough. The end result of selfishness is frustration and emptiness. A selfish woman actually works against herself. Selfishness blocks her attempts to gain what she wants. Did the person in Isaiah 14:13-17 get what he wanted?

10. One of Jesus' familiar teachings is one of the most misunderstood passages in the Bible. Read Matthew 5:3-12 in the light of the Scriptures you have just studied. In what area of your life will you take a step of selflessness and humility today?

❧ *WISDOM'S PATH* ❧

There is a sort of musical score for living the Christian life. All of us are expected to play this composition. We have different instruments and have been assigned various parts, but we are all to be playing the same composition.

The name of the composition? Well, it's not exactly popular. In fact, you hardly ever hear it sung or played. The title is "The Way to Up Is Down." The words of this composition can be found in Philippians 2:5-11. (Biblical scholars call this passage the *kenosis* passage, after the Greek word translated, "made Himself nothing" in verse 7. *Kenosis* literally means "emptied.")

The musical score begins with emptying and ends with exaltation. It ranges from modesty to majesty. It provides us with an example to follow—the example of Christ's humility.

Self-acceptance. Notice that Jesus began with self-acceptance. "Who, being in very nature God, did not consider equality with God something to be grasped." Jesus knew who He was—God in His very nature. He did not spend His life trying to find Himself. If we have not discovered our identities in Christ, we will be continually frustrated. The search for oneself, apart from a union with Jesus Christ, results in a selfish, pride-filled lifestyle. It is only in Him that we find ultimate fulfillment. If we are in Christ, we can accept ourselves, because God has accepted us, and we can move on toward humility.

Self-forgetfulness. Jesus did not cling to His equality with God. He released His grip on Himself. Jesus let go of the rights and privileges that were legitimately His as He turned from Himself to consider the needs of the world He had come to serve and to save. Many of today's "successful" people achieved their present fame, wealth, or success by being self-promoting, shrewd, and oblivious to the people they stepped on to get where they are. But, self-forgetfulness is to be the model among the people of God.

Self-denial. Jesus made Himself nothing. He emptied Himself. He denied Himself. Self-denial is essentially the ability to free oneself from the bondage of personal desires and needs. Instead of directing one's own life, self-denial gives up that direction to God. Instead of depending on yourself to find fulfillment, self-denial turns to God with a desire for His blessing and direction.

Selflessness. Christ went a step beyond self-denial, "He took the very nature of a servant, being made in human likeness." Servanthood is losing oneself in the service of another. However, in reality, servanthood is a self-preserving way to love oneself. "Whoever loses his life for my sake will find it" (Matt. 10:39).

Humility. Jesus' humility was clearly demonstrated in His obedience to God, obedience that resulted in His death on a cross. Ironic as it may seem, humility is the biblical form of positive self-esteem. It is characterized by accurate self-appraisal, responsiveness to the needs of others, and a willingness to give praise to others before claiming it for oneself. Do you see these characteristics exhibited in Jesus' humility? Before claiming praise for Himself, Jesus was willing to provide grace for us. To provide that grace, it was necessary for Him to experience death—the most humiliating death known to men of His time, death on a cross.

Earlier I said that our musical composition ranged from modesty to majesty. There is not much majesty associated with death on a cross. But there is majesty associated with servanthood. The majesty associated with servanthood is not self-manufactured, but God-bestowed. In Philippians 2:9-11, Paul sums up the life of Christ on earth:

> Therefore God exalted Him and gave Him the name that is above every name, that at the name of Jesus every knee should bow, in heaven and on earth, and under the earth, and every tongue confess that Jesus Christ is Lord, to the glory of God the Father.

Christ's entire life was an illustration of the teaching He often gave His followers: "Whoever wants to become great among you must be your servant" (Matt. 20:26).

The discipline of humility means denying, disowning, and crucifying everything in us that is incompatible with Jesus Christ. At the same time we are to affirm and value all that is Christ-like in our newly created selves. Humility leads us from the point of saying "all of self and none of Thee," to "some of self, and some of Thee," to "less of self and more of Thee," to "none of self and all of Thee." As C.S. Lewis once said, "If you meet a truly humble man, he won't be thinking about humility; he won't be thinking about himself at all."

❧ DAILY PILGRIMAGE ❧

SUNDAY: Matthew 5:3

God says

I respond

MONDAY: Zephaniah 2:3

God says

I respond

TUESDAY: 1 Peter 5:5

God says

I respond

WEDNESDAY: Matthew 18:12

God says

I respond

THURSDAY: James 4:10

God says

I respond

FRIDAY: Proverbs 16:18

God says

I respond

SATURDAY: Isaiah 57:15

God says

I respond

CHAPTER SEVEN

THE DISCIPLINE OF

❧ PERSONAL JOURNEY ❧

Read Proverbs 16.

1. The secret to feeling comfortable with one's use of time is *planning*. Planning is not wrong. It does not demonstrate a lack of faith or trust in God. Planning is essential for good stewardship, and stewardship of time is commanded in Scripture. What do the following verses say about our responsibility in planning? What do they say about God's role in our planning?

   Proverbs 16:1

   Proverbs 16:3

   Proverbs 16:9

2. According to Proverbs 16:2, what is the most important factor in our planning? (What does the Lord consider?)

3. "Motives" are the underlying purpose for planning and doing what we do. All good planning begins with a clear statement of purpose which becomes the focus of our goal-setting.

Read Philippians 3:7-11. Summarize Paul's motivation or purpose in life.

4. Goal-setting is the discipline of deciding on specific ways to accomplish one's purpose in life. The following verses contain some important advice to follow when setting goals. Summarize the advice given in each.

Proverbs 16:3

Proverbs 16:7

Proverbs 16:20

5. "Priorities" refer to the values that help us determine the order of importance of goals and daily activities. Sometimes our choice is clearly between good and evil. At other times, we must choose between the "good" and the "best." Identify the choices called for in the following verses. Circle the action or attitude that is most desirable.

Proverbs 16:8

Proverbs 16:16

Proverbs 16:19

Proverbs 16:22

Proverbs 16:32

6. Once a person has determined the priorities in her life, it is time to make specific plans to achieve them. Identifying the time, place, and necessary equipment needed to achieve the goal will prepare you for taking concrete steps toward it. This may require some research and personal observation. What do Proverbs 16:20, 22 say about the role of education in achieving your goals?

7. Following through on the specific actions you have decided on is all that remains to complete the planning process. What does James 4:17 say about the person who does not do the good he knows he should do?

8. First Corinthians 14 gives instructions about planning orderly worship services. These principles also apply to the planning of our lives and the use of our time. Summarize these two verses:

1 Corinthians 14:33

1 Corinthians 14:40

9. Read Romans 12:1-2. What steps should we take to know and understand God's will for us?

10. Complete this statement:

My purpose in life is to

11. What goal in each of the following areas will help you come closer to fulfilling your purpose in life?

    Relationships

    Health

    Vocation

    Personal growth

    Financial

    Spiritual

12. Choose one of the above areas to work in this week. What is it?

13. What action could you take toward reaching that goal today?

♣ WISDOM'S PATH ♣

Some people seem to spend more time planning a party or summer vacation than they spend in planning their lives. This should not be so among Christians who take the Word of God seriously.

> Live life, then, with a due sense of responsibility, not as men who do not know the meaning and purpose of life but as those who do. Make the best use of your time, despite all the difficulties of these days. Don't be vague but firmly grasp what you know to be the will of the Lord (Eph. 5:15-16, PH).

Do you ever feel like you don't have enough time to get everything done? If you do, then one of three things might be causing the problem: you might be doing too much; you might be doing the wrong things; or you might be doing the right things the wrong way. The time you invest in planning will be worthwhile. Just as it takes money to make money, it takes time (planning time) to make time.

Planning begins with a statement of one's purpose. Can you summarize the general purpose you have in life? Write it down. Someone has said, "The palest ink is stronger than the strongest memory." A written statement of life purpose is like a lighthouse toward which you can direct your goals and actions. It will keep your life from becoming fragmented and cluttered by unimportant and unrelated efforts.

After identifying your purpose in life, you are ready to begin setting goals for the various areas of your life. It is good to have a sense of priority about these areas. My priorities include (in order of importance): my spiritual life, my relationship with my husband, my children, my relationships with the members of the body of Christ, outreach to the lost, and miscellaneous (vocation, hobbies, education, etc.).

Now establish the order of your priorities and write down some long-term goals. What would you like to have accomplished at the end of 5 or 10 years? A study done recently showed that 10-year goals that were written down were usually accomplished within 2 years! There is great value in writing goals down.

Next, write down a smaller goal (short-term) that will take you one step toward achieving your long-range goal. In setting these goals, make sure they have these four characteristics:

□ *A deadline.* What is the date by which you need to accomplish this goal?

□ *A measurable quality.* How will you know when you get there? Don't just say, "I will lose some weight." Say, "I will lose 10 pounds by the end of the month."

□ *A challenge.* Each goal that you set should be one step beyond others you have taken. Remember: It is better to aim for a star and hit a mountain than to aim at a mud puddle and hit it every time.

□ *Realism.* It would be unrealistic and discouraging to set a goal of losing 40 pounds in a week. Be realistic about the goal you set so that you have a better chance of achieving it.

Now you are ready to establish a plan of action. Define the goal in detail. Set a deadline to complete your plan of action. Write down the steps you will take. Identify the supplies you need and make sure you have them before beginning the task. Estimate the time you will need to accomplish the task and set a start-up time that will help you meet your deadline.

Once the action plan is complete, you are ready to begin. If you are a procrastinator, refer to the study on the discipline of energies (chapter 3) to overcome the urge to procrastinate. Remember: Action is necessary to move your goals and plans from dreams to realities.

Once you have completed your action plan, review the results. There is an internal pleasure we gain from work well done. God experienced this at the end of His creative work. He looked at all He had made and it was good. If you didn't quite meet the goal, readjust your action plan, not your goal. Then follow through on your new plans.

These steps, if followed, will give you the satisfaction of following the example of the ant in Proverbs 6:6-11. This passage encourages us to work hard and plan to meet the needs of the future. The story of the ant illustrates these principles of time management: Know what to do, know when to do it, and be a self-starter.

What sets a Christian woman apart is the unique perspective she brings to her planning and time management. By yielding herself to God, refusing to be conformed to the pattern of this world, and by renewing her mind through a study of God's Word, she can know and do His will (Rom. 12:1-2). Then her priorities, goals, and planning will reflect God's will.

The will of God is never contrary to the Word of God. There are some goals and activities that are never appropriate for a Christian. On the other hand, there are some attitudes and actions that are *always* appropriate for a Christian. A growing Christian will share David's desire: "Teach me to do your will, for you are my God; may your good Spirit lead me on level ground" (Ps. 143:10).

A practical tool that I have found helpful in organizing my life and managing my time is an 8½" X 5½" loose-leaf notebook. Several years ago after reading Anne Ortlund's book, *Disciplines of the Beautiful Woman*, I began my notebook adventure. As a result of the success I experienced in getting my life more organized, I self-published my notebook. It is now helping several thousand women become more self-disciplined in the area of planning.

The main dividers of the note book are: Goals and Agenda, Christian Disciplines, Ministry, Home and Family, Personal Enrichment, and Journal. My notebook combines several different organizational tools. It is a bulletin board, a calendar, an address book, a coupon holder, a menu planner, a prayer journal, a Bible study notebook, a diary, and a budget book all in one cover. It helps me remember things. This takes some of the pressure off of me to remember everything. It helps me balance my schedule and evaluate how well I am using my time. It records answered prayer, personal inspiration, and daily happenings. It is an idea book and a source of creative outlet. It also helps me save money as I discipline myself to plan menus and maintain a list of *needs* and *wants*.

The notebook is not magic. It is a method. You may find another method that works for you. Ask God for wisdom to know the best approach to managing your time for serving Him.

❧ *DAILY PILGRIMAGE* ❧

SUNDAY: Proverbs 6:6-8

God says

I respond

MONDAY: Proverbs 13:4

God says

I respond

TUESDAY: Ephesians 5:15-20

God says

I respond

WEDNESDAY: Luke 10:40-42

God says

I respond

THURSDAY: Ecclesiastes 3:1-8

God says

I respond

FRIDAY: Matthew 11:28

God says

I respond

SATURDAY: Philippians 3:13-14

God says

I respond

CHAPTER EIGHT

THE DISCIPLINE OF

Financial Management

🎵 PERSONAL JOURNEY 🎵

Read Proverbs 22 and 28.

1. Money is one of the most important topics in today's world. How to get it? How to spend it? How to keep it? And how to get more of it? These are the major questions of the secular world. However, the emphasis of the Bible is not "How can I get money?" but rather "What is my attitude about money?" In this study, we will consider what God has to say about improper attitudes toward money.

   One improper attitude is greed. Study these verses about greed. Summarize what they have to say.

   Proverbs 15:16-17

   Proverbs 15:27

   Proverbs 23:4-5

   Luke 12:15

2. Describe the wise reaction to the ungodly attitude of greed spoken of in Proverbs 22:9 and 28:25, 27.

   In his book, *Money, Sex and Power*, Richard Foster says that the act of letting go of money, or any other treasure, destroys greed. When was the last time you gave away something of value to yourself?

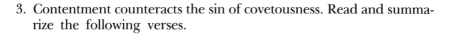
3. Contentment counteracts the sin of covetousness. Read and summarize the following verses.

Philippians 4:11

1 Timothy 6:8

Hebrews 13:5

4. Another inappropriate response to money is ignorance. Summarize what the following verses have to say about money management.

Proverbs 14:15

Proverbs 15:22

Proverbs 19:2

Proverbs 20:18

Proverbs 24:3-4

5. Impatience is a dangerous attitude when it comes to money management. An impatient, get-rich-quick attitude is typified by excessive borrowing to purchase items that are not in line with one's financial earnings or status. List the dangers associated with the desire to get rich quick. Refer to Proverbs 20:21; 21:6; 28:19-20, 22.

6. The proper responses to impatience are trusting God to provide financial resources, and living as faithful stewards of what we *do* have. Summarize the following verses.

Matthew 6:19-21

Matthew 6:31-34

1 Timothy 6:17-19

Proverbs 28:20

Proverbs 22:7

7. What money matter is most pressing in your life right now?

Are you struggling with any improper responses to money? Which one?

What steps do you plan to take to discipline your attitudes about money?

🐦 *WISDOM'S PATH* 🐦

Let me tell you where I'm "coming from." Some of you will identify with our family. Others will not. Though it is hard for me to admit, we live comfortably when compared with many other families in our country. It's hard to admit that because too often I compare my life with those who have more, rather than those who have less.

Though I must say we are comfortable, it does get a little tight now and then. Sometimes I wistfully wonder what it would be like to be able to make decisions without always needing to know the cost involved.

I share my financial profile with you so that you will understand why I am still reeling after reading *Money, Sex and Power* by Richard Foster. I have always heard that money is neither good nor bad; it is the *love* of money that is evil.

> Challenge #1. Foster contends that money is *not* morally neutral. Rather, it is a power that seeks to dominate us.
>
> Challenge #2. I used to think that only rich people could be guilty of loving money. Now I see that we poor and middle-class people are in as much (or more) danger of worshiping at the altar of money.

I'm glad that I have been forced to do some thinking on this subject. Jesus thought it was so important that except for the kingdom of God, He addressed this subject more than any other. His teaching was usually not directed at only the rich or only the poor. The principles He espoused apply to everyone.

The principle of stewardship. Matthew 25:14-30 is the Parable of the Talents. This parable presents several principles of stewardship.

☐ God is the sovereign giver. We are entrusted with His property.
☐ He expects us to handle and invest the trust wisely.
☐ We will be held accountable for how we handle the trust.
☐ Faithfulness with a small amount results in being entrusted with more.

The principle of priority. The sayings of Jesus on this principle need no commentary.

> Do not store up for yourself treasures on earth, where moth and rust destroy, and where thieves break in and steal. But store up for yourselves treasures in heaven, where moth and rust do not destroy, and where thieves do not break in and steal. For where your treasure is, there your heart will be also (Matt. 6:19, 21).

Adopting the priorities that Jesus taught will give us happiness that all the money in the world could not offer. The formula for true wealth is found in 1 Timothy 6:6:

Godliness + Contentment = Great Gain

Contentment is learned. Keeping your priorities in line with those Jesus advocated will keep your life on track. Eternal priorities continually remind us that "we brought nothing into the world, and we can take nothing out of it" (1 Tim. 6:7). As Charles Swindoll once said, "I never saw a hearse pulling a U-Haul trailer!"

Most of us need to learn to appreciate and accept the basics of life, by commiting ourselves to a simpler, less affluent lifestyle, "If we have food and clothing, we will be content with that" (1 Tim. 6:8). Simplifying our lifestyles will help us learn contentment.

The principle of giving. A third principle that Jesus taught is that we should be givers. Jesus spoke of the widow who gave out of her poverty. Her gift was acceptable though small. In God's sight, it was "more" than the other gifts because it represented a larger percentage of the total wealth of the giver. In Matthew 19:21 Jesus instructed a rich man, "If you want to be perfect, go, sell your possessions and give to the poor, and you will have treasure in heaven. Then come, follow me."

Giving requires an act of the will which disengages the power that money would seek to exert on us. It strikes a blow to the greed that drives us to hoard our possessions and wear ourselves out getting more. Giving is not a "gift" reserved for the materially rich person. The following insights from 2 Corinthians 8 are based on the premise that rich and poor alike can benefit from giving:

☐ Generosity is not based on the amount of the gift but the heart of the giver.

☐ Acceptable giving begins with a gift of one's self to God.

☐ God is not so much concerned with what we give away as with what we keep for ourselves.

☐ We should always be ready to give to the needs of others.

These wrong attitudes need to be replaced by godly responses. Greed can be overcome by generosity and giving. Covetousness must be replaced by a content spirit. Ignorance can be overcome by obtaining wisdom, understanding, and instruction. Impatience can be replaced by trust in God's timely provision. Indulgence can be replaced by thriftiness.

Paul concluded his first letter to Timothy with words that apply to all of us who are rich in comparison to the rest of the world (almost anyone who had the money to buy this book):

> Command those who are rich in this present world not to be arrogant nor to put their hope in wealth, which is so uncertain, but to put their hope in God, who richly provides us with everything for our enjoyment. Command them to do good, to be rich in good deeds, and to be generous and willing to share. In this way they will lay up treasure for themselves as a firm foundation for the coming age, so that they may take hold of the life that is truly life (1 Timothy 6:17-29).

🍂 *DAILY PILGRIMAGE* 🍂

SUNDAY: Matthew 6:31-34

God says

I respond

MONDAY: 1 Timothy 6:6-11

God says

I respond

TUESDAY: 1 Timothy 6:17-19

God says

I respond

WEDNESDAY: Proverbs 23:4-5

God says

I respond

THURSDAY: Luke 12:15

God says

I respond

FRIDAY: Hebrews 13:5

God says

I respond

SATURDAY: Proverbs 15:16-17

God says

I respond

CHAPTER NINE

THE DISCIPLINE OF

Friendship

❧ *PERSONAL JOURNEY* ❧

Read Proverbs 27.

1. List five characteristics of one of your good friends.

2. Look up and read the following verses. Summarize the qualities that contribute to friendships found in each verse.

Proverbs 27:5

Proverbs 27:6

Proverbs 27:9

Proverbs 27:10

Proverbs 27:17

3. Do the qualities you have listed above describe casual acquaintances or intimate friends?

4. Proverbs 27 is filled with advice on "how-not-to" be a friend. In the following verses, what actions or attitudes destroy friendship.

Proverbs 27:1

Proverbs 27:3

Proverbs 27:4

Proverbs 27:5

Proverbs 27:6 (implied)

Proverbs 27:10

Proverbs 27:14

5. Certain characteristics should typify relationships among Christians. Read the following verses and list the characteristics of a Christian relationship. (Hint: look for the phrase "one another.")

Romans 12:10

Galatians 5:13

Ephesians 4:2

Ephesians 5:21

Colossians 3:13

1 Thessalonians 5:11

James 5:16

1 Peter 4:9

6. Have you ever been guilty of being too busy to be a good friend? Maintaining a friendship is a little like playing catch with a ball. It is impossible to play catch if one person refuses to throw the ball back. In the same way, friendship cannot progress if one person repeatedly "holds the ball." How have you reciprocated, or tossed the friendship ball back to someone in the past seven days?

7. Read John 15:12-17. What was Jesus' command to His friends?

8. How did Jesus demonstrate His love for us, His friends?

9. What does it mean to "lay down your life for your friends?"

10. To forego personal desires to meet the needs of a friend is not an easy thing to do. Disciplining yourself to do so, however, will bring great rewards (see Luke 6:38). What do you want to do for a friend in the next few days?

🍂 *WISDOM'S PATH* 🍂

Recently I attended a mother-daughter buffet where the theme was "Friends Forever." The event was a delight, from the teddy bear decorations to a skit involving a dialogue between two young teens at a slumber party. A slide presentation accompanied by music and script showed friends from the church engaging in various activities: touching, talking, playing, and praying.

The highlight of the evening was when three women shared their experiences of special friendships. For one woman, a middle-aged widow, her special friend was a woman who was available to help care for her children and relieve the pressures of single-parenting. This friend remembered the widow's wedding date and had a special party for what would have been her twenty-fifth anniversary. The friend "shared" her husband to do small maintenance jobs around the house. Most of all, this friend listened and loved, and sensed the needs of her friend.

Another young woman told of a friend who baby-sat for her children while she and her husband partied and caroused. Never preaching, this friend prayed and waited for the right time to speak of Christ and His love to this couple. Eventually, the love of this friend led to the salvation of the young woman and her husband.

Marsha (not her real name) told of a friendship that began while her husband was in graduate school. She formed a friendship with another graduate student's wife. The friend gave birth to twins during their school years. One of the babies was found to be mentally handicapped. The handicapped baby was so fussy that only her mother and Marsha could handle her. Marsha often relieved her friend so she could get out of the house. The two friends spent hours together laughing, crying, sharing budgeting secrets, and taking their five preschoolers for walks in the park. After graduation, they were separated by hundreds of miles. Frequent letters and annual reunions were the vehicles of their friendship. One day Marsha received a letter from her friend saying that she had joined a cult and no longer wanted contact with Marsha. Marsha's tears and expressions of love and concern for this friend and her family, in spite of the rejection, were evidences of true friendship.

Each of these women had experienced the kind of friendship for which all of us yearn. I was reminded that evening of some special friendships I enjoy. Each friendship is a little different. I thought about the different levels of friendship that exist. On each level there are different and appropriate interchanges that are necessary for maintaining the friendship. Think about your friendships. See if you can determine what levels of friendship you have experienced.

Acquaintance (someone to talk to). Friendship at this level is characterized by spasmodic personal contact. Each of us has the potential for many friendships at this level. It has been said that a man who would have friends must show himself friendly. This is easier for some people to do than others. Have you ever envied someone who is at ease among a group of strangers? Through self-discipline you can learn to meet people more easily. Here are a few skills to develop:

☐ Think of some general questions to initiate conversation with strangers.

☐ Ask your questions in such a way as to reflect genuine interest and acceptance.

☐ Learn and remember names.

☐ Remember that God is concerned for every person. Know that even new acquaintances are made by divine providence.

Casual (someone to play or work with). Friends at this level share interests and activities. Discussions should be centered around observations or common interests. Ask your questions in such a way that you will gain insight into their hopes and dreams. Show interest and concern if these friends share a problem with you. Demonstrate trustworthiness by not violating any confidence they place in you. See if you can observe where they are in their relationships with God. Talk to God about them and their needs.

CASUAL/Close (someone to count on). Casual/close friendships are based on mutual trust. As you get to know a person better, you should begin to think of even more questions to ask. Be on the lookout to discover the person's strengths. At this level of relationship you should be honest about yourself and acknowledge your weaknesses when appropriate. Demonstrate your trust and appreciation for this friend-ship.

Casual/CLOSE (someone with whom to share mutual experiences and special times). Friends at this level share general life purposes. You can ask questions regarding the other's life purpose and share your own. As a good friend, you should be able to identify potential in the other person's life. You can ask about her specific goals and encourage your friend to reach her goals. As you come across Scripture that would encourage her and guide her, share it with her. Friendships at this level are described in Ecclesiastes 4:9-10, "Two are better than one, because they have a good return for their work: If one falls down, his friend can help him up. But pity the man who falls and has no one to help him up!"

Close (someone with whom to share thoughts and ideas). This level of friendship is based on similar goals. There is freedom in this relationship to suggest mutual projects to help each other achieve goals. In fact, close friends share some of the responsibility for the development of their friend's life and goals. Friends at this level discuss their thoughts and ideas without fear of ridicule or rejection.

Intimate (someone to trust who will respect and support you and your growth). Notice how the number of friends declines with each level of friendship. The person who experiences friendship at the intimate level has cause for real rejoicing. Intimate friendship is based on a commitment to the development of each other's character. There is freedom to point out and correct each other's character deficiencies. Honesty and discretion are important for maintaining an intimate friendship. Intimate friends comfort one another through difficulties, assume responsibility for the other's reputation, and commit themselves to loyalty and availability. Intimate friends become sensitive to characteristics in themselves that need improvement, and invite their friends to tell them about their faults. Together they can search the Scriptures and pray for solutions to problem areas.

Maybe you have not spent a lot of time analyzing friendship. It is better to spend you time enjoying your friendships! Analysis is helpful, however, if your desire to become a better friend or to increase the number of friendships you have. If you look closely you still observe several elements common to all relationships: conversation, comfortableness with silence, sensitivity, thoughtfulness, genuineness, willingness to spend time in each other's company, and concern.

🍂 *DAILY PILGRIMAGE* 🍂

SUNDAY: Psalm 119:63

    God says

    I respond

MONDAY: 1 Samuel 18:9

    God says

    I respond

TUESDAY: Romans 13:10

    God says

    I respond

WEDNESDAY: 1 John 1:7

God says

I respond

THURSDAY: Ecclesiastes 4:10

God says

I respond

FRIDAY: Ruth 1:16

God says

I respond

SATURDAY: 2 Timothy 1:16

God says

I respond

THE DISCIPLINE OF

CHAPTER TEN

❧ *PERSONAL JOURNEY* ❧

Read Proverbs 28.

1. One of the most loved verses in the Bible is Proverbs 3:5. Write it in the space provided below.

2. To trust God with one's *whole heart* is a life-long discipline. Trusting with my whole heart means that I cannot depend on anything other than God. The Bible speaks of many other objects of trust that interfere with trust in God. Look up and read the following verses. What false objects of trust are described in each verse?

   Psalm 20:7

   Psalm 44:6

   Psalm 118:8-9

   Proverbs 11:28

   Proverbs 28:26

3. Think about yourself and the people you know. In what "things" do modern men and women trust?

4. Can you think of an example from your life that would show how untrustworthy these things are?

5. The Bible is full of statements about the faithfulness of God. Read each of the verses below and write out every phrase that assures you that you can trust Him.

   Deuteronomy 7:9

   1 Thessalonians 5:24

   2 Thessalonians 3:3

   Hebrews 13:5

   Hebrews 13:8

6. The Psalms reveal that David trusted God for the same reasons that we can: who God is and what He has done for us and for others. Look up each of the following references and then list them in the

appropriate columns. Psalms 9:10; 22:4; 22:9; 44:6; 55:23; 56:3; 62:5-7; 68:5-6; 68:20; 77:11; 90:1-2; 95:3-5; 103:8; 104:27; and 120:1.

Who God Is	What He's Done for Others	What He's Done for Me

7. Read the following verses and write down the benefits of trusting God found in each verse.

   Proverbs 16:20

   Proverbs 22:19

   Proverbs 28:25

   Proverbs 29:25

   Proverbs 30:5

8. Trusting God requires action and is demonstrated by confident living. Philippians 4:6 gives some good advice on how to begin trusting God. Summarize the advice of Philippians 4.

9. What will be the inward manifestation of one's trust in God? Read Philippians 4:7.

🦋 WISDOM'S PATH 🦋

Do you think of trust as an active or passive trait? For many years I thought of trust only in a passive sense. I thought trusting God referred to a kind of laid back approach to life. This made it difficult for me to trust God because I am not a laid back sort of person.

Lately I have come to see that trust is not a "what-will-be-will-be" attitude. Rather, trust is a disciplined activity of the mind that results in bold action. The following acrostic outlines the mental discipline involved in trusting God:

> **T**hink
> **R**emember
> **U**nderstand
> **S**ubmit
> **T**hanksgiving

Think. To put one's faith in God is not to stop thinking. Some people assume that following Christ means giving up the capacity and desire to think for yourself. That is not true. Some of the most brilliant people in the world are Christians. In our generation we have seen Christians penetrate almost every area of professional life. Government, sports, education, and research are only a few of the areas in which Christians are having an influence.

Perhaps you see yourself as I see myself—a rather ordinary, simple person. However, thinking is just as important a part of trusting for us "ordinary" people as it is for a genius. Peter said that his letters were written to make people think (2 Peter 3:1-2). He tells us to think about the words of the prophets and the commands of Christ. That is an excellent place to begin. Like David who meditated on the law of the Lord, we should become hearers, readers, thinkers, and doers of the Word of God.

Memorize Philippians 4:8. This verse gives us good guidelines for our thoughts. Discipline your mind to broaden your knowledge and your ability to trust God.

Remember. Most of the psalms are songs that either praise or describe God's trustworthiness. In times of trouble, David would recall God's faithfulness in past circumstances. Establishing a personal bank of God's faithfulness will give you a reserve from which to draw in hard times. David and Karen Mains introduced this concept into their family with the "I Spy" notebook. They suggest keeping a daily record of the evidences of God at work in your life.

The psalms also record God's specific acts of faithfulness to others. David wrote of God's provision for the Children of Israel in their days in the wilderness. It is encouraging to read the Bible with an eye to spying God at work. Be alert to observe and remember God at work in the lives of people in the past as well as people around you.

Understand. There is one very important thing to understand:

> "My thoughts are not your thoughts, neither are your ways
> my ways," declares the Lord. "As the heavens are higher
> than the earth, so are my ways higher than your ways and
> my thoughts than your thoughts" (Isa. 55:8-9).

Proverbs 3:5 tells us not to lean on our own understanding. Although we are to use all our abilities to think and reason, we are to keep a proper perspective. Our ability to think and reason is extremely limited and dull when compared to the wisdom of God. Understanding our limitations is an important part of trusting.

Submit. "In all your ways acknowledge Him." I have often dutifully quoted this verse, having only a foggy idea of what it meant. For some people, "acknowledging God" seems to mean saying a good word for the "Man upstairs" or a hurried prayer before a meal. However, acknowledging God means recognizing His authority. In all my ways I am to recognize and submit to His authority. Submission is not a popular concept, yet we submit every day to people we have never met! When we keep the law, we are submitting to lawmakers and law enforcers. When we pay the list price for an item, we submit to the manufacturers and store owners. But submission gets a little tougher when we deal with people we know.

Our inability or unwillingness to submit to another person may indicate a lack of trust in that person. Unwillingness to submit to God in any area of life indicates a lack of receptivity to His perfect love. "Perfect love drives out fear" (1 John 4:18). There is no reason to resist the authority of God who loves us. When we are secure in His love, we will submit to Him in trust.

But we never can prove the delights of His love
Until all on the altar we lay;
For the favor He shows, And the joy He bestows,
Are for them who will trust and obey.
Trust and obey, for there's no other way
To be happy in Jesus,
But to trust and obey.

—John H. Sammis

Thanksgiving. A fifth action in developing the discipline of trust is to express thankfulness to God. Paul said, if we want to experience God's peace, we should not be anxious about anything, but present our prayers and petitions to God with *thanksgiving* (Phil. 4:6). "Give thanks in all circumstances, for this is God's will for you in Christ Jesus," (1 Thes. 5:18). Giving thanks in all circumstances means giving verbal support to an inner attitude of confidence we have placed in God.

No matter what your circumstances, it is time to trust God in all areas of your life. *Think* on His Word. *Remember* His faithfulness in the past. *Understand* that His ways are perfect and higher than human comprehension. *Submit* to His lordship. *Thank* Him in all circumstances.

Those who hope in the Lord will renew their strength. They will soar on wings like eagles; they will run and not grow weary, they will walk and not be faint (Isa. 40:31).

TRUST IN HIM.

☙ DAILY PILGRIMAGE ☙

SUNDAY: Psalm 37:3-5

    God says

    I respond

MONDAY: Psalm 62:8

    God says

    I respond

TUESDAY: Isaiah 12:2

    God says

    I respond

WEDNESDAY: Psalm 56:3-4

   God says

   I respond

THURSDAY: Psalm 125:1

   God says

   I respond

FRIDAY: Nahum 1:7

   God says

   I respond

SATURDAY: Isaiah 26:3-4

   God says

   I respond

❧ *LEADER'S GUIDE* ❧

The following leader's guide provides you with specific suggestions to facilitate group discussion. You will find it most helpful if you encourage people to do the study before the group meeting. The objectives of this study are: first, to acquaint people with what the Bible actually says; and second, to show how the Bible applies to the practical problems of modern life. Go over the questions in class. Encourage discussion, but try to keep the discussion centered on the lesson, avoiding tangents. Remind group members that the more time they spend studying the lesson, the more interesting and informed the discussion will be.

As each session comes to a close, help group members discuss and draw conclusions that are practical and applicable to their individual problems. Also spend time sharing and praying for each other. This will increase the benefit each group member gains from this study.

&. *LEADER'S GUIDE 1* &.

Objective
To help group members identify ways to find and apply God's wisdom to life's daily situations.

Personal Preparation
☐ Complete the *Personal Journey* section of chapter 1. Jot down questions that come to your mind as you study Proverbs 1–4.
☐ Read *Wisdom's Path*. Try to think of situations in your own life where you need God's wisdom to cope.
☐ Look for an example of ungodly counsel in a newspaper or a magazine you have access to. Take the example to your group meeting to use as an illustration.

Group Participation
☐ Let the group share their answers to question 1 of the *Personal Journey* section. Come up with a group definition of *wisdom*.
☐ Point out the differences between God's wisdom and worldly wisdom. Ask group members to share examples of each. This would be a good time to show the newspaper or magazine article you brought with you. Ask: **Where have you heard or read unwise counsel in the past week?**
☐ Ask group members to recall past occasions when they needed God's wisdom to get through difficult situations. Ask some group members to share their experiences with the rest of the group.
☐ Discuss the various problems that one might encounter during different stages of personal and/or family life.
☐ Emphasize that our quest for God's wisdom leads us to a *place* (God's Word) and a *person* (Jesus Christ).
☐ Let group members give examples of how God's Word has changed their lives.
☐ Ask members to discuss their answers to question 11 with the rest of the group.
☐ Spend time praying for one another. Ask group members to pair up and pray for God's wisdom.

🍂 *LEADER'S GUIDE 2* 🍂

Objective
To heighten awareness of the problems associated with infidelity. And to bring group members to a renewed appreciation of their marriages.

Personal Preparation
☐ Complete the *Personal Journey* section of chapter 2. Make a note of your observations on the Scripture passage.
☐ Read *Wisdom's Path*. Ask God what you can do this week to make your marriage even happier. Be on the lookout for related material to supplement your group study.

Group Participation
☐ Spend some time discussing question 1. Ask several group members to share their comparisons of the two approaches to life.
☐ Ask: **Where are extramarital affairs made to look glamorous?** Discuss the dangers of exposing ourselves to influences that portray infidelity in a glamorous light.
☐ Ask group members to read the following verses: Genesis 3:5; Matthew 4:6; 2 Corinthians 2:11; and 2 Corinthians 11:14. Then discuss the ways that Satan seeks to deceive and ruin people.
☐ Ask: **Why are the consequences of an action not enough to keep people from sin?**
☐ Discuss the young man in Proverbs 7:7-23. Ask: **Do you think he was innocently wandering through the streets that evening? Why do you think he was taken in by the gaudy, loud woman?**
☐ Discuss the analogies in Proverbs 7:22-23. How was the young man like an ox, deer, and bird?
☐ Ask group members to share some of the blessings they have experienced as a result of their marriages.
☐ Share with the group some of the most refreshing times you and your spouse have had together.
☐ Ask: **What resources have you found helpful in strengthening your marriage?**
☐ Close with a time of silent prayer.

❧ *LEADER'S GUIDE 3* ❧

Objective
To challenge group members to overcome procrastination, laziness, and unfocused activity through the discipline of energy.

Personal Preparation
☐ Complete the *Personal Journey* section of chapter 3.
☐ Read *Wisdom's Path*. Think of a time when you procrastinated. How did you feel? How did you finally overcome it?

Group Participation
☐ Share examples of procrastination. Ask group members to suggest areas in which they tend to procrastinate.
☐ Discuss question 2. How does the ant demonstrate principles of time management?
☐ Discuss the statement: "You don't *do* what you do because you *feel* like you do. You *feel* like you do because you *do* what you do."
☐ Ask the group for their impressions of the woman of Proverbs 31. What did they discover in their studies of that passage?
☐ As a group, think about what the woman of Proverbs 31 would be like if she were alive today.
☐ Spend time praying for one another, especially for needs relating to the discipline of personal energy.

🍂 *LEADER'S GUIDE 4* 🍂

Objective
To help group members establish as priorities, a daily quiet time and a quiet spirit.

Personal Preparation
☐ Complete the *Personal Journey* section of chapter 4.
☐ Read *Wisdom's Path*. Plan for and observe a time of personal quietness before the group meets. Be ready to share your experience with the group.

Group Participation
☐ Answer questions 1 and 2 as a group.
☐ Ask: **What are the benefits of spending times of silence with God?**
☐ Ask group members to share their answers to question 5.
☐ Discuss the part that quiet times played in the life of Christ.
☐ Discuss how there must be a balance of quiet periods in our lives to offset the hectic schedules that we must meet.
☐ Use the following story to get a discussion started. **In spite of mothering a large number of children, John and Charles Wesley's mother found a way to have her quiet time. She would retreat into a corner and put her full-length apron over her head. In this position she was able to observe a time of quietness and prayer, in spite of what was going on around her!** Ask group members what difficulties they encounter when trying to get alone. How are they able to overcome them?
☐ Ask: **How will the discipline of quietness help alleviate some of the symptoms of stress?**
☐ Discuss the differences between the four disciplines of quietness that are mentioned in *Wisdom's Path:* silence and solitude, listening to God, reflection and meditation, and prayers of worship and intercession.
☐ Tell those who would like to observe a period of quietness to sign their names to a slip of paper. Then have group members exchange names and pray for one another during the week.

🦜 *LEADER'S GUIDE* 5 🦜

Objective
To alert group members to the importance of controlling their words.

Personal Preparation
☐ Complete the *Personal Journey* section of chapter 5. Jot down related questions and thoughts as you study Proverbs 15.
☐ Read *Wisdom's Path*. Be alert for situations that would illustrate the importance of controlling your speech.

Group Participation
☐ Ask several group members to share their answers to question 1.
☐ Help the group come up with some guidelines for judging speech by reading them the following questions: **Before I say anything I should ask myself, "Is it the right time?" "Is there something I should say?" "Is there something I should not say?"** Ask them to come up with criteria for answering these questions in different situations.
☐ Have group members pair up. Then assign a chapter from Proverbs to each pair. (It doesn't matter what chapter). Tell each pair to do a "treasure hunt," looking for references to the tongue or speech in their chapter. After about ten minutes, bring the group back together and have someone from each pair summarize their findings.
☐ Have someone read 1 Thessalonians 5:11 aloud. Then have the group weave a "love web." As the leader, you begin by picking one person in the group and telling her what trait you admire in her. Then, take a roll of toilet paper and hand it to the woman you picked, allowing it to unroll as you continue to hold on to the end of the roll. She should then repeat the process, holding the toilet paper and unrolling it as she passes it to the person she compliments. If the women enjoy this activity, you may repeat it for several rounds around the group.
☐ Have several members lead in prayer. Express thanksgiving for one another and for the gift of speech.

🍂 *LEADER'S GUIDE* 6 🍂

Objective
To exalt Christ who demonstrated ultimate humility and to encourage group members to pattern their lives on His example.

Personal Preparation
☐ Complete the *Personal Journey* section of chapter 6.
☐ Read *Wisdom's Path*.
☐ Make sure you are clear on the definitions of pride and humility as they are used throughout the study.

Group Participation
☐ Spend some time discussing the meaning of pride. What kind of pride is not evil? What kind of pride should have no place in the Christian's life? Try to come up with a comprehensive definition of pride.
☐ Ask: **What are some of the results of sinful pride?** Refer them to the verses in question 2.
☐ Ask: **Can you think of modern-day situations that demonstrate any of the pitfalls of pride?**
☐ Discuss question 3. Ask: **Can you think of a particular instance in the life of Christ when He demonstrated that He knew and accepted who He was?**
☐ Ask: **Can you think of a time in the life of Christ when He could have risen to political power, or achieved some other claim to fame, but chose not to?**
☐ Ask: **How did Christ demonstrate His selflessness?** Ask the group to suggest several times when He served others without concern for Himself.
☐ Discuss opportunities you and your group members have for displaying selflessness on a day to day basis.
☐ Ask the group to agree or disagree with this statement: **A selfish person does not love himself or herself enough.**
☐ Close by asking group members to look at their responses to question 10. Have a short time of silent prayer for each person to reaffirm her commitment to that action.

✿ *LEADER'S GUIDE 7* ✿

Objective
To help group members increase their time-management skills and to identify and plan for a personal goal.

Personal Preparation
☐ Complete the *Personal Journey* section of chapter 7.
☐ Read *Wisdom's Path*. Design and carry out your own action plan as described in *Wisdom's Path*. This action will give you a base from which to share experiences during the group meeting.

Group Participation
☐ Discuss question 1. Ask: **Is any of the responsibility for planning removed from us since God is in control of everything?**
☐ Discuss the differences between purpose, goals, priorities, and planning.
☐ Ask if anyone would like to share their purpose in life. If someone responds, compliment them for their effort to condense their thoughts into a statement of purpose. Ask them what they learned from this exercise.
☐ Ask several women to share their answers to question 5.
☐ Ask group members to decide on one goal and develop an action plan to reach that goal. Then have them write their action plan out on a slip of paper and exchange papers with another group member. Encourage the women to pray for one another during the week. They might wish to phone the person they are praying for, to encourage them to positive action.
☐ Close in prayer.

❦ *LEADER'S GUIDE 8* ❦

Objective
To assist group members establish habits of financial discipline that will result in a lifestyle consistent with the teaching of Jesus Christ.

Personal Preparation
☐ Complete the *Personal Journey* section of chapter 8.
☐ Read *Wisdom's Path*. Make a note of questions that come to your mind.
☐ Collect enough secular magazines to provide one for each person at your group study. You will be analyzing advertisements.

Group Participation
☐ Distribute the magazines you brought. Ask group members to tear out two or three advertisements that appeal to them.
☐ Ask group members to suggest the ungodly responses to money they discovered in this study. Ask them to name any other ungodly responses that were not mentioned in the study.
☐ Ask: **How would you describe greed?**
☐ Tell them to lood at the advertisements they selected from the magazines. Ask: **Which advertisements promote greed?**
☐ Discuss what the wise response to greed is. Ask: **Why is it hard to give things away? Why would we rather have a garage sale, for instance?**
☐ Ask for a definition of "covet." Discuss the difference between greed and covetousness.
☐ Ask: **Do any of the advertisements encourage covetousness?** Discuss your answers.
☐ Encourage discussion on the topic "How to be content."
☐ Ask: **Which advertisements invite you to make a rash, impulsive decision? What is the remedy to impatience and impulse buying?**
☐ Close in prayer asking God for wisdom in handling the money and other resources with which He has entrusted us.

🍂 *LEADER'S GUIDE 9* 🍂

Objective
To help each person be a better friend and develop better relationships.

Personal Preparation
☐ Complete the *Personal Journey* section of chapter 8.
☐ Read *Wisdom's Path*.
☐ Purchase a box of stationery notes (enough for one note for each group member).

Group Participation
☐ Ask group members to think of Bible characters who had very good friends.
☐ Compile a list of the qualities of a good friend from answers to question 1.
☐ Ask: **What are some of the investments you must consider when making a new friend? How do you move from one level of friendship to another?**
☐ Discuss the ways to destroy a friendship from question 4. Ask the group to think of some others to add to the list.
☐ Review the list of "one anothers" from question 5. As you go through the list, discuss practical ways to do each one.
☐ Ask: **To whom was Jesus a friend?**
☐ As a group, compare what you know about Jesus with the list of qualities that make a good friend. How does He rate?
☐ Discuss what it means to "lay down your life for your friends." Ask: **What are some practical ways we can apply this?**
☐ Distribute the stationery note cards. Ask each person to write a brief note of appreciation to a friend.
☐ If appropriate, try singing these words to the tune of "Row, Row, Row, Your Boat": *I have found a friend / Very special friend / Loving, caring, kind, and true / Jesus is my friend.*
☐ Close with short, sentence-length prayers, thanking God for friendship and the best friend, Jesus.

🍂 LEADER'S GUIDE 10 🍂

Objective
To help each group member advance to a deeper level of trust than she has previously experienced.

Personal Preparation
☐ Complete the *Personal Journey* section of chapter 10.
☐ Read *Wisdom's Path*.
☐ Try keeping an "I Spy" notebook as described in *Wisdom's Path*.
☐ Identify an area of your life in which you need to develop the discipline of trust.

Group Participation
☐ Begin the session by quoting or reading Proverbs 3:5-6.
☐ Ask: **What things stand in the way of our trusting God with all of our capacities?**
☐ Have group members share examples of when these "things" proved to be unworthy of trust.
☐ Ask several group members to share their answers to question 5 with the group.
☐ Ask group members to share their answers to question 6. First talk about who God is; then what He's done for others; then what He's done for me.
☐ Ask: **What are the benefits of trusting God?** (Refer to question 7.)
☐ Allow about 10 minutes at the end of your session to compose a psalm of trust. Have each person contribute a line that begins with the word, "When . . ." and ends with the phrase, "I will trust in God." (E.g., When I don't understand why my mother has cancer, I will trust in God.)
☐ Read the completed psalm to conclude the session. If you can, make copies to distribute to each person as a reminder of this study.
☐ Close in prayer.